LATE

Also by Cecilia Woloch

Sacrifice (1997)
Tsigan: The Gypsy Poem (2002)

LATE

Poems by

CECILIA WOLOCH

AMERICAN POETS CONTINUUM SERIES, NO. 80

BOA Editions, Ltd. • Rochester, NY • 2003

07 08 09 4 3 2

Publications by BOA Editions, Ltd.—
a not-for-profit corporation under section 501 (c) (3)
of the United States Internal Revenue Code—
are made possible with the assistance of grants from
the Literature Program of the New York State Council on the Arts,
the Literature Program of the National Endowment for the Arts,
the Sonia Raiziss Giop Charitable Foundation,
the Lannan Foundation,
as well as from the Mary S. Mulligan Charitable Trust,
the County of Monroe, NY,
Ames-Amzalak Memorial Trust,
and The CIRE Foundation.

See Colophon on page 80 for special individual acknowledgments.

Cover Design: Greg Boyd
Cover Photo: Thomas Lux
Cover Art: "untitled" by Jonde Northcutt, courtesy of the artist
Interior Design and Composition: Richard Foerster
Manufacturing: McNaughton & Gunn, Lithographers
BOA Logo: Mirko

Library of Congress Cataloging-in-Publication Data

Woloch, Cecilia, 1956–
    Late : poems / by Cecilia Woloch.
        p. cm. — (American poets continuum series, v. 80)
    ISBN 1–929918–42–9 (pbk. : alk. paper)
    I. Title. II. Series.

PS3573.O5677L38 2003
811'.6—dc22

                                                          2003057870

BOA Editions, Ltd.
Nora A. Jones, Executive Director/Publisher
Thom Ward, Editor/Production
Peter Conners, Editor/Marketing
Glenn William, BOA Board Chair
A. Poulin, Jr., President & Founder (1938 - 1996)
250 North Goodman Street, Suite 306
Rochester, NY 14607
www.boaeditions.org

In Memoriam

Harry Woloch, Jr., 1925–1998
JoAnn Lawton Bealmear, 1925–2000

Contents

III.

LATE

And how many twilights there are there,
And shadows, and how cool it is . . .

—Anna Akhmatova, "The Reader"
(tr. by Judith Hemschemeyer)

Love is not changed by Death,
And nothing is lost and all in the end is harvest.

—Edith Sitwell, "Eurydice"

I.

Aubade

Now the trees stand outside of desire, stricken with silver, stripped leafless, alarmed. Still they long to be seen, throw themselves skyward with open arms. Just as the earrings—obsidian—gleam where they lie, having longed to be taken off. Not to be rid of themselves, but to hint at undressing, dalliance. Oh brilliance of being a beautiful thing in a world full of beautiful things. In which even suffering shimmers and means. In which even the lover's absence pools in the shadows at my feet. I can step back from the window or not. I can choose to be just as lovely without ever being watched. As the bare trees make cradles for birds. As he once cupped the black, tear-shaped jewels in his palm. Oh world, hold us up to this light. There is so much to lose that we haven't lost.

Bareback Pantoum

One night, bareback and young, we rode through the woods
and the woods were on fire—
two borrowed horses, two local boys
whose waists we clung to, my sister and I

and the woods were on fire—
the pounding of hooves, the smell of smoke and the sharp sweat of boys
whose waists we clung to, my sister and I,
as we rode toward flame with the sky in our mouths—

the pounding of hooves, the smell of smoke and the sharp sweat of boys
and the heart saying: *mine*
as we rode toward flame with the sky in our mouths—
the trees turning gold, then crimson, white

and the heart saying: *mine*
of the wild, bright world;
the trees turning gold, then crimson, white
as they burned in the darkness, and we were girls

of the wild, bright world
of the woods near our house—we could turn, see the lights
as they burned in the darkness, and we were girls
so we rode just to ride

through the woods near our house—we could turn, see the lights—
and the horses would carry us, carry us home
so we rode just to ride,
my sister and I, just to be close to that danger, desire

and the horses would carry us, carry us home
—two borrowed horses, two local boys,
my sister and I—just to be close to that danger, desire—
one night, bareback and young, we rode through the woods.

Hades

Where we go when he closes my eyes
and under what country:
some blue darkness, farther than hell;
a landscape of absence and root and stone.
There are no bodies here,
we dream shapeless dreams—
a constant, cloudless storm.

Mother, I'll never wake up from him,
I have already traveled too far.
My mouth is the color of his mouth
and his arms are no longer his arms;
they're mute as smoke, as my first white dress,
and the spear of his name, once ferocious,
dissolves on my tongue
like sugar, like birdsong, I whisper it:
Hades.

My Mother's Birds

My mother's Polish nickname was the word for "dried-up"; *sticks—Sucha*, her mother called her. *Little witch; Miss Skin-and-Bones*. Fifth of eleven thin and startled children, all those mouths to feed. Okay: it was the Great Depression; everyone was poor. They baked potatoes over fires in the street, my mother said; dipped stale bread in buttermilk, *ate what was put in front of them*. And she was dark-eyed, dreamy, danced in vacant lots, played movie star. Tied her black hair up in rags; high-kicked through cinders, broken glass. Picked cigarette butts from the gutters for the pennies *Dzia-dzia* gave. Though *CioaCia* Helen down the hill, their crazy aunt, was better off. She gave them sweets, cheap sweets but sweet. She gave them Easter chicks one year. My mother took the tiny peeps and raised them tenderly, as pets. I've seen the photographs: their white wings all aflutter in her arms. As if such chickens could have flown, but they were meat, those birds she loved. Tough meat, and these were hungry years. And CioaCia raised the axe. My mother sobbed and couldn't swallow, nor could anyone, I've heard. The story goes she saved a few stray feathers, hid them, sang to them. Knelt above them weeping in the attic, *just like church*. Fed and watered them for months, her sisters laughed; *the ghosts of birds*. The way, years later, always singing, she would try to fatten us. Her own strange brood of seven children, raised less tenderly, perhaps. As if, this time, she wanted to be sure we'd get away. She'd set the steaming plates in front of us, still humming, cross her arms. *Don't be afraid to eat,* she'd say, because we were. We were afraid.

Blink

I was small and I believed I could disappear
just by closing my eyes—
as many children believe,
but I wished for it fervently:
that my scarred hands, red with itch,
would become the ghostly hands of saints;
the dark oval of my face dissolve,
transparent as the air.
How does a child fit a body she hates?
How does a child learn to hate what she is?
At school I was *wool-locks, chink-eyes, freak*;
each slur a rich disfigurement,
some trapped thing spat back, maimed.
In church, the gravest of my sins
in the hushed confessional: *this flesh*
which, bead by bead, I prayed might be illumined, changed, erased.

Oh I would have died to be beautiful once
—Saint Cecilia, Saint Genevieve—
wrapped myself in the scratchy sheets
to be buried, and risen again;
to blink and vanish—look:
here's how the world turns a girl on the wheel of herself,
what wasn't murdered in me:
a face that stares back from the glass of its longed-for death,
alive, and loves what it sees.

Après la Lune de Miel

Those first mornings, I swooned in my sleep, woke damp with your breath, was not bitter yet. From our windows we watched the neighbors collect in small congregations of gloom: the men wearing black woolen suits; the women who followed them, kerchiefed, heads bowed. That couple whose child seemed to grow more enormous, more horribly plump every day; how they pushed her—their burden, their gift—in the grim pram in front of them, stared straight ahead. We looked down and laughed at their somberness. Thought we were blessed, high above them, apart—having no history, no angry gods.

That was a time called *la lune de miel*: moon made of honey, sky made of milk. Then the thin blue of paradise slipped from our arms. Then I bit down on your fingers and wept, having dreamt of you gouging the bread from my mouth. Then our garments—once frivolous, bright—hung themselves by the shoulders and sobbed in the dark. And I began practicing, night after night, how best to leave you, whose sleep was a shroud. Offering prayers to the flickering shapes, to the shadows of flame on the walls of that house. I was learning self-discipline, wakefulness, flight. I would sit until dawn with the windows flung wide, naming our children, escaping from them.

Shemoneh 'Esreh

the silent or whispered part of a prayer

And those evenings, our neighbors—Jews, Hasidim—
could have watched from their windows till dawn
my shadow moving by candlelight, seen

had they risen, gazed out, that I rarely slept:
that the man lay in bed while the woman, awake,
bent to some furious task at a desk—

it would not have looked like prayer to them,
though sometimes I bowed there, murmured, wept;
it would not have looked like worship then,

though sometimes I knelt in my window's lit cage,
tiny flame cupped like a bird in my hand.
And sometimes the building our building faced

blazed all night with arguments, chairs on the lawn;
but I kept a quiet house—radiant, hushed—
they would not have reckoned

someone had shattered there; someone still ached to be born.
Theirs was an old country, dim as a ship
weighted with dark psalms, and I was a girl;

I was a penitent, too, still a bride
with a small book of saints at my hip, with a hymn
I hummed over and over again through those nights

with the ash of his kiss on my tongue, with the ash
of his kisses on my breath.

Slow Children at Play

All the quick children have gone inside, called
by their mothers to *hurry-up-wash-your-hands*
honey-dinner's-getting-cold, just-wait-till-your-father-gets-home—
and only the slow children out on the lawns, marking off
paths between fireflies, making soft little sounds with their mouths, *oh*s
that glow and go out and glow. And their slow mothers flickering,
pale in the dusk, watching them turn in the gentle air, watching them
twirling, their arms spread wide, thinking, *These are my children*, thinking,
Where is their dinner? Where has their father gone?

Beauty

How lackluster the world would be if we didn't die.
—Holly Prado

I.

I decide finally to leave the house in late afternoon, when the sun's less harsh. When Los Angeles, parched with heat, starts to drink its own shadows, forgive itself. I drive five miles to the canyon to walk; park on a side street. Get out. Breathe. The air's turned tawny and cool by now; people are hiking here, walking their dogs. I take the trail skyward, as high as it goes, through scrub and brush, past gnarled manzanita, the whisper of sea grass, then turn to look: the city in miniature, spread at my feet; the first lights of evening blinking on. The horizon is streaked with rose, shot gold; a jet cuts through clouds in a silver arc. I think how my father will miss this world. I think of how we can't kill beauty, how beauty can't be killed. It's nearly dark by the time I walk down. A woman ahead of me, swinging her arms.

II.

We're hanging new curtains tonight. Two of my friends have come to help; they're drilling holes in the walls for the curtain rods and it's taking a while to get right. So we decide to stop and eat. I call for some Indian carry-out. When the bell rings, I dash downstairs with a handful of cash to pick it up. The delivery boy is a fair-skinned female, just about my age. I tip her and notice a shopping cart parked in the street, heaped with bottles and rags; another heap next to it, piled on the curb. Upstairs, my apartment seems vacant, fresh, with all the windows bare. We're passing the curry around the kitchen table when red lights start to flash. An ambulance. Blue lights. Police. We look out to see what's going on. The heap of rags has become a woman who has fallen into the street. The cops are trying to talk to her, trying to get her to come along. The paramedics have pulled out a stretcher;

they've gathered around her and lifted her up. "It's cold out there," one of us says. "They're taking a lot of time with her." When I look again, later, the street is empty, even the shopping cart is gone. My friends finish hanging the rods and I hang the curtains, lovely and sheer. "This way, the sky will come in," says Ed. Who is Ed? Who is anyone?

III.

At 2 A.M., I switch on the computer to check for messages. I'm expecting a note from my mother: the report about my father's condition she sends me every night. The blank screen blinks then fills with text. *We had to laugh,* I read. *He was finally awake. He was yelling my name.* My father who's lain for days in the ether of sleep between life and death. *He pinched us when we were trying to clean him up. We had to laugh.* I smile and type out a reply: *I'm glad you're having a little fun.* I think of my father lashed down in that bed, shrunken and bent: half bird, half man. How they've covered the mirrors with sheets so he won't have to see himself like this. How my mother and sister lean over him, turning him, bathing him, laughing out loud. How he kisses the hand that dabs at his mouth, calls *LaVerne, LaVerne,* whispers *beautiful.*

Ottava Rima: Lear

Perhaps we ought to be ashamed and aren't
of Daddy lying helpless in that room,
tethered to the bed, and frail and bent,
who was God as in Our Father once but whom
we bathe like our own child and kiss and pet
and introduce to strangers we bring home
as if he still might rise up like a king—
white-haired, wild-eyed, fearless, welcoming.

My Mother's Pillow

My mother sleeps with the Bible open on her pillow;
she reads herself to sleep and wakens startled.
She listens for her heart: each breath is shallow.

For years her hands were quick with thread and needle.
She used to sew all night when we were little;
now she sleeps with the Bible open on her pillow

and believes that Jesus understands her sorrow:
her children grown, their father frail and brittle;
the stitches in her heart, her breathing shallow.

Once she *even slept fast,* rushed tomorrow,
mornings full of sunlight, sons and daughters.
Now she sleeps alone with the Bible on her pillow

and wakes alone and feels the house is hollow,
though my father in his blue room stirs and mutters;
she listens to him breathe: each breath is shallow.

I flutter down the darkened hallway, shadow
between their dreams, my mother and my father
asleep in rooms I pass, my breathing shallow.
I leave the Bible open on her pillow.

Last Words

While he was dying, I sat at the foot of my father's bed reading Rukeyser's poems. He was asleep or he was awake. I looked up occasionally and, occasionally, I thought I saw him smile. Thought there was something he wanted to say. But language had flown from him by then. Language had fallen onto the pages in my lap, like snow, like ash. The other rooms in the house that spring were full of human sound—loud conversation, TV news, kids banging doors running in and out—but in that room at the end of the hall, it was quiet, just the three of us: the dead poet, her work in my hands; my dying father; my own caught breath. I read through tears, sometimes, and sometimes just stopped reading and stared into space. The way my father seemed to be staring out from the half-dream of his death. Where was the world we could open and close with a touch, the mind quick as a startled bird? I looked down at the words on the page, read them silently, read them again: *When I am dead, even then . . . I will wait for you in these poems.* Who was speaking then, and to whom? *I am still listening to you.*

Pour Vivienne

C'est l'heure, little wren,
  little shadow on horseback,
    wing of black hair,
      little Vivienne.
C'est ton père—
  like a bell being rung:
    C'est ton père, c'est ton père.
      Il est mort, Vivienne.
What must your mother
  have said meaning
    gone and *forever*,
      your father, your prince?
How must the news have struck
  when she woke you to tell you:
    son coeur
      s'est arrêté—?
In which language
  can such words be spoken
    and not break the spell
      of the sleeping child?
Leur princesse,
  sur son cheval cheri.
    And how will you run again,
      small vivid one?
Long-legged,
  smelling of grass,
    pony and miracle,
      wild rush of sun—
as he dreamed of you,
  dreamed of you once,
    as he dreams now
      flying over the field.

All Hallow's Eve

How far apart are we then?
The bell struck says *Father*—two syllables
hang in the air, then the ghost
of the echo: *he's dead.*
I stand here thinking: *What separates us?*
The glass in the frame I kiss
and beneath it the photograph of a man
who passed through this world in a body, a shape
—*who passed away*—to where?

All Hallow's Eve: so the distance thins;
it's said they come nearer to us, the dead.
So we light candles, ring bells, we turn
at the window, the breath of the night on our arms.
Who giveth? Who taketh away?
What did he mean when he waved and waved,
saying, *Hope for the best,*
never spoke again?

Nocturne

only night heals again
  —H.D.

H.D., there are birds in the trees
just outside my windows I've never seen
though they call to each other all night
under cover of darkness: *Give us this branch;*
give us this branch, small wings, this sky
and deliver us singing to ourselves.
The ruined world still holds, the ruined world
still harbors nightingales, mockingbirds, still
harbors the bobwhite my father whistled to
when I was a child, he was whole.

And now our cities bleed light, stain the sky
with neon rosiness, blurring the stars;
and our fathers grow old and die
but some go on singing, some sing even now,
though nothing replaces what everyone's lost:
the strict constellations, the bright map above
the girl sprawled in summer grass ticking them off—
the names of the planets, the heroes and gods—
her father beside her, invisible, calm.

When I was that child I believed in trees
as leafy ghosts, and in holy birds;
and I believed in the dark earth turning
at our backs, the wheel of sky.
I was afraid of this world, even then,
but I loved it, too, as I loved him.
What is the source of such music, H.D.?
Where do we go when we die, when we sleep?
You, who have reached out to me like a branch,
like the pale arm of god,
you must know why we sing.

After World

And, as for eternity, what's that
but the collation of all the hours we have known
of sweetness

and urgency
                                      —Mary Oliver

Where the world ends in moonlight and falling stars, I have tried to call you back from the dead. Where the white cliffs drop off into clouds and, beneath them, the green over green of your grave, I have wished for a word, some sign, one glimpse of your face in the dream of grief. Where the black of the sky gives way to the nothing of night, just your hand on my hair—I've begged for that mercy of touch, but the gods don't hear; there are no gods. Your ghost in the silence of trees will not weep, though I know you would take my hand. At the end of the world, you would stand beside me, saying, *This is my daughter*, still. And I would not be afraid to be stepping from that edge into the wind.

II.

The Passionate Suitcase

I fall out the door on my way to you, and the passionate suitcase—the old one, so many times strapped back together—comes unstrapped. The leather ties slap at my calves like tongues. The five silver dollars I got from my uncle for spelling *Mediterranean Sea* roll along the ground. I believe the moon blinks. Once.

I fall out the door on my way to you one terrible night and the passionate suitcase unhinges its mouth the way children sob. My clothes lie in puddles at my feet. Pools of rice, pools of soft lingerie. Which is more than the traffic of leaving; more than I'd wanted to kneel, gather up.

I fall out the door on my way to you with the passionate suitcase I've carried so long flapping its one broken arm in the breeze. It spills all the words in the street like coins. The words for *desire* and *regret*. I fall out the door on my way to you. The night slams shut. I don't look back.

Red Curtains

As one walks in darkness past a house
suffused with radiance, and the curtains pulled . . .
Still I would be outside each separate world . . .
                                        —Ann Stanford

I.

The heavy red curtains drift in the breeze, billow and sigh
in the open window of my neighbors' upstairs bedroom.
Someone is taking a nap in there—no, someone
has just gotten up and is washing her hair. It's late afternoon;
the smell of shampoo wafts out toward me on the solemn Sunday air.
A dog barks. A man's voice says *No*, very clearly, then *No* again,
hushed—one long breath—and I think I hear the word *hips*
and press my spine against the stucco wall where I'm sitting, envious,
alone on my porch in the alley while all around me the open windows
of my neighbors fill with dusk. There are whole lives going on inside:
lovemaking, meals being planned, dogs trained to sit and beg
at the threshold, to wait for the gesture that blesses, forgives, the *yes*
that means *yes, you may come in; we will love you, too,*
we will lie down, soon, again. There is no such thing as death.

II.

The second man I ever loved was *a gem.*
He liked to go walking in early evening past
the houses just being lit, to glimpse
through those jewel-bright windows other lives
he longed to live. He was living alone
in a few cheap rooms; we were students then.
He liked to lie down and read aloud to me
from fairytales, children's books; to watch
me sleep (he told me this) the nights I slipped
out of the women's dorm to share his narrow bed.
He called me *Sugar*; cooked our Sunday dinner
on two blue rings of flame, sighing, *Sugar,*

you know I'd die for you. And I knew
those nights he would. His body was luminous,
pale as a summer storm. His hair was red.
That June, he pawned his violin
to take me dancing; was *a prince.*
I have never been sorry I loved him, never
sorry I left him, too. Though he wanted marriage,
children, *a home,* he said—a life I couldn't
offer him, or wouldn't. So I gathered up my notebooks,
wept a little, stepped out blessed
into the darkly gleaming world.

III.

Wind-hole: an opening then.
In the solemn, anguished evenings of the marriage
I finally made (unmade again, unwound,
like a skein of bandages stained red—
how many loves that failed, how many
wounds to kiss, to bless?) we'd leave the house
at dusk each Sunday after dinner,
hand in hand, stop beneath our neighbors' windows
just to sigh, breathe in
those lives the heavy curtains hid;
to *covet (cupidus, cupere; also: akin to vapor, smoke)*
their quiet rituals, the way their lit shapes
moved from room to room;
to practice death, then, being ghosts.
We'd stand outside in wind, in shadow, while the world within grew
    bright.

IV.

And ever since, the windows glow, holy
of holies, gold with light. *Why
have you never married again?*
I married once; that was enough.
One hard season of glittering chance. I've missed

37

his laugh, sometimes, the way he'd fill
an ashtray with his change. We smoked.
We waited for something like *desire*
to descend again. He left red roses
on my desk. And when I packed my books, the habits
of my solitude, and went, I wept
for days: *my home, my home.*
Since then he's found a house on a quiet street;
another wife. A woman I'm told
could be your twin. I've dreamt of her;
I've driven past that place our ghosts made love
and blessed its emptiness.
I've meant *surrender* when I've said
forgiveness, too. *You'll die alone,*
some suitor warned. And so will you.
(And something moves the curtains, breathes into the room.)

V.

To live alone, to stand outside
those windows, haloed, breathing light
and still to want the only door
(which some call *love*: that entering.)
But I have never craved the red
of being kept, the heavy draperies
of *this will be enough.*
I've lain down some.
I've risen up like smoke
and turned my back and dressed.
I've left those rooms and walked
the wind-blessed streets and felt
my own shape pass:
    Beloved, other, not my life—
you are within the world and then
you step away, you just go on.

Filth

I love the filth of Paris, I love Paris in its filth. Even stepping off at Passy, into the elegant *Sixteenth*, I can taste the soot in the air; a black curtain billowing after the train. And later, a woman offers me petits fours—pretty petits fours on a plate—and I love how she pulls her dainty chair away, lights a fat yellow *Gitanes Maïs*. How the gilded room goes blue with smoke and the woman dissolves in it, crossing her legs.

And I love the café "Le Chien Qui Fume" on Boulevard du Montparnasse. How the light is yellow, worn, and the waiter's shirt has not been ironed. And "La Petite Chaumière" in the crooked, damp Marais where we've come for fish. How we heap the bones on a plate, the oily heads, the thin gray skin. And how my friend insists on paying, *but there is nothing romantic in this.* On the street, I blow him kisses, step over dog shit, laugh out loud.

And in the station at Hôtel de Ville, there's a couple across the tracks. The man sitting down in an orange plastic chair, the dirty blonde facing him, straddling his lap. She is kissing his forehead again and again; he closes his eyes and lets her kiss. Her sweater slips out of the waist of her jeans, exposing the small of her back to us: a seam of pasty, naked flesh; the elastic band of her underpants.

I get off the metro a few stops early to walk up the Champs-Élysées in the rain. A drunken man shouts from a telephone booth; police sirens wail down the boulevard. And I swear a woman is squatting to pee between parked cars just below the Étoile. She's wearing a mink coat, stockings and pumps; has a small cocker spaniel on a leash. I want to shout, "*Bravo, bon courage!*" as she totters away just ahead of me.

Paris is beautiful like this; it's the beauty of love of the body of love. Once I arrived here in winter, alone; smelled bread and tobacco and butter and piss. And what had, until then, been my heart was not so much broken as opened in sin.

Forty-three Rue de Saintonge

There was a book full of fallen leaves that had not been read
There was a chance
There was a chair near a window, a lamp
There was a sky of hammered tin with a few thin clouds in it, some birds

There was a chance
A noise in the courtyard like rain, and rain, and the clatter of keys
There was a sky of hammered tin with a few thin clouds in it, some birds
And several clocks at once and, everywhere, bridges, a river like smoke

A noise in the courtyard like rain, and rain, and the clatter of keys
A stairway being climbed in both directions, curved and steep
And several clocks at once and, everywhere, bridges, a river like smoke
There was a taxi moving slowly through the streets, the city blurred

A stairway being climbed in both directions, curved and steep
A door behind which jazz was playing softly, candles burned
There was a taxi moving slowly through the streets, the city blurred
A rosary of longing being fingered, bead by bead

A door behind which jazz was playing softly, candles burned
And little tongues of flame cast into mirrors and thrown back
A rosary of longing being fingered, bead by bead
Dusk: the curtains gathering their shadows, and a bed

And little tongues of flame cast into mirrors and thrown back
There was a chair near a window, a lamp
Dusk: the curtains gathering their shadows, and a bed
There was a book full of fallen leaves that had not (that still has not)
    been read

And Here's to You, Jesus Robinson

for Wilfried Merkel

I have to imagine him there: maybe four or five years old, in a small German village, just after the war. A red-haired German boy with that look in his eye that he has even now. Even now, as he tells me the story of how he met Jesus Robinson. A single moment remembered some fifty years later. Surprised. And innocent.

My friend was the youngest of seven boys. Five of his brothers would grow to be priests; the two little sisters were yet to be born. One of those girls would commit suicide. His parents would live to be old, live through this, as they'd lived through the war. They had sent him away to the countryside as so many children were sent. To stay with a grandmother or an aunt till the worst was over. Perhaps it is.

Perhaps he is already learning to laugh at the wild contradictions of being alive. So many men have died in their uniforms, maybe it hurts to be young. Maybe it hurts him to squint, look up into the sun when these new men arrive. Men in other uniforms, now, but soldiers as well: the Americans. I think he is serious, though, this boy. I think he's a grave and serious child who has not tasted chocolate in all the war.

And he's never seen men who look quite like these men who pass through the streets of the small German town. Men who wave down at him from the tanks, tossing sticks of chewing gum, careless smiles. Maybe he doesn't smile back, but I bet that he does. I bet that he raises one shy hand and returns the strange gesture: *Hello, Good-bye.*

And how must he look to them, from their terrible height, as they ride their machines? Machines that could crush the frail shops and houses, the small boy who waves up at them from the street. Machines that could crash through the world he has known until now, which has always been falling down. The boy is small, even small for his age. Do they see his flaming hair in the sun? Do the soldiers think, as I have thought myself: *If I'm looking for an enemy, I will not find him here.*

The boy stares up into a face unlike any face he's seen before. The skin is creamy, lustrous, dark; like the pictures in schoolbooks of Africans. Like the paintings in museums if there are any paintings left. And the boy would like to taste this face, to touch this skin, to know its name. The man is laughing; something gleams in his right fist. A coin, perhaps. Gold as the treasure of lost ships and now it's glinting, falling fast. Falling toward the boy who stands amazed with upraised palms.

Then perhaps the man leans back and places both hands on his hips. So that his shadow falls across the red-haired boy who shades his eyes. Who reads the name stenciled over the pocket, and mouths it: *Jesus Robinson.* Then peels the foil from the melting coin, lays the sweet disc on his tongue.

He'll never forget that face, he tells me, wide-eyed, white-haired now. How sunlight fell into his hands; how darkness melted on his tongue. How a man named Jesus Robinson stopped the war inside him once.

Dzien Dobry

*Exile is an uncomfortable situation. It is also a
magical situation.*

—Hélène Cixous

In Rzepnik—a village
of maybe twenty families
strewn across hillsides, fields
on the banks of the river
named Merk, as in "Dark,"
in the lower Carpathians (*end
of the world*): each house
with its weary cow, its chickens
scratching the dirt in the yard;
each window its white
lace curtains; each morning
its light—in *the glorified
shed* my friends call
home (bare floors
swept with a broom made
of twigs; bathwater heated
at night on the stove)—
where I woke late
one spring day, having dreamt
through the clamor of church bell
and bird-cry, alone,
into absence and hush
(*where had everyone gone?*)—
the front door ajar and the fire
unstirred; the faint hum of flies
buzzing over the wreckage
of breakfast—half-eaten
apple, brown bread, tin of fish—

where I had grown thin
on a diet of grief, unspeakable
consonants caught
in my throat; no word

from my love in that far
other world, nothing
in weeks that did not
taste of ash—and, sighing
put on the kettle to boil
(*rat in the well last year*)
rinsed out my cup, then,
sensing someone behind me, turned
to whoever had entered
(*no murmur, no knock*)
and waited in silence:
the neighbor, Kasczyk—

a man I'd watched bent
at his work in the fields
and thought: *I know nothing*,
some book in my lap—strange
to these villagers, strange
to myself—lost,
with no language
to speak to him now
as he stood in that shimmer
of sunlight and dust, boots
caked with mud, body
worn as a blade
—almost transparent—
fresh eggs in his hands:

the shells tinged
with blue and still warm,
I could tell, by the way
he was holding them, cupped
in his palms, the moment
I felt him there—(*shift
in the air*) in my stubborness,
bitterness, *terror of filth*—
and facing him, wordlessly,
nodded my head.

Dobry, he said,
at last: *good*, and was gone—
only sun on the table,
his gift of fresh eggs.
Dzien, I called out
to the bright, empty room—
having meant to say
thank you, dziekuje,
and said only *dzien*, only
day, for *dzien dobry*,
good day—when I woke
to the grace of *eat that
which is offered*, knew,
in that light, where to turn.

Proposals

Mistaking me for someone else, he asked me to marry him. This has happened more than once. The first time, I was eighteen and the boy had a diamond ring in a box. It was the Fourth of July, it was dark, he said, *Happy Independence Day.* Of course, the ring was too large and slipped right off my finger into the grass. (It belonged to someone else: the woman he married, eventually.) And when I was twenty-one, that redhead, sloe-eyed and slinking out of his grief, said he'd imagined I'd be his wife. But he was mistaken. It wasn't me. Then a drunk who drove too fast, who threw the proposal over his shoulder like some glittering, tattered scarf. I staggered out of his car, saying, *No thanks, No thanks, No thanks.* And the man over eggs one morning, in the midst of an argument, saying he planned to wait for spring *to ask for my hand,* then he never asked. (So of course, I married that one for a while; spent years convincing him I was *not his cup of coffee,* not his girl.) And in Prague, on a bridge called the Karlův Most, a stranger, a refugee, who mistook the way I stared at the river for thinking of suicide. Who mistook my American passport for his ticket out of there. And others—the man whose children grabbed the food off my plate, called me *her;* the man in Chartres Cathedral humming the wedding march into my ear. And tonight, at dinner with friends, happy, discussing their wedding plans, a man I've known for a couple of hours turning to ask me to marry him. I don't know who they think I am. Do I look like a bride in these rags of wind? Do I look like the angel of home and hearth with this strange green fire in my hands?

Grass Widow

a discarded mistress

—Webster's Dictionary

She lies down in meadows, alone—
lies down in high grass, abandoned, lies down
among wildflowers, weeds, will not weep—wants the sun
which lies down across her to hold her there, warm
the sweet earth beneath her—a grave she might love
if, having been cast off, she wanted to die.

The River Esk

Dark as the love that lays us low
    —Kelly Cherry

The river says *hush* and I think of you crying out, calling my name in the act of love. Your face in the darkness, pale, where it looms above me—changing, changed. Your pleasure so deep that it looks like pain. (What is *torture*? What is *desire*?) The river says *shh*, and you let yourself slip into that current, gasping, sigh. Oh love, in the act of love you are mine and not mine—shining, drowned. If the river says *cliff* and *far* and *dive*, will you fall through this distance toward me, plunge? It's been thousands of miles since we met at the mouth, at the hip, in the river that calls to us—*come*.

Lasswade, Midlothian: Dusk

Crow, I cried, *I need to talk to you.*
The whole sky lurched.
Black wings. Most bitter trees
I've ever seen. Wild daffodils.
Here is a world
that is just as the world was world
before we named it *world*.
Here is a sky that screams back at me
as I rush toward it, darkening.

"Whose Shadow Has Been Lifted like a Mute Veil from the World"

—Dabney Stuart

You wanted me to go everywhere, do everything, be brave. You wanted that sickly little red-eyed girl, your daughter, to grow strong. Bury her heartaches as she went and also live with them. I have. I've dragged my grief across the map you spread out tenderly, and look: I'm facing a window facing a river facing cliffs you never saw. I'm growing old in the world unfolding you had wanted me to love. The way you loved it, even dying in your bed, gasping and mute. From where I'm sitting, I can taste the wind: I'd offer this as breath. Just breathe again. Just make a wish among the dark trees. Be here, too.

III.

Custom

Some days you wake up and find god in your shoes and you don't know who put it there. Or the little gold clocks in your irises, or the long stems of sun on your desk. So you just dress in coffee and beautiful rags and be glad of it, ashes and all. And you hum to yourself some ridiculous tune that sounds like a handkerchief stuffed in your mouth. Which means that you won't get a single thing done, oh no not today, but your papers don't mind. They lie around like wanton brides and admire you anyway. Fat apples blossom in baskets left on your table; wine turns into wine. And the windows, my god the windows have gathered absurd amounts of sky. *If the shoe fits, the foot must be mine.* Someone who loves you dreamed double last night.

The Hammock

We've driven all day to get here—
Robert steering the Olds with one hand
from L.A. to San Francisco and now
I'm stretched out in Jorge's hammock
where he left me, on the porch,
having begged me, *Lie down, rest,*
said I looked tired, then came back,
wrapped me in the quilt from his own bed.
No stars tonight, but there are clouds;
I watch them cross the blue-black sky,
just watch and listen—from the kitchen
at my back, men's voices, soft:
Jorge's voice and Robert's voice
and the sounds of chopping,
chopping, talk of vegetables and sex.
I hear them speaking of childhood gardens,
what they ate but did not love
and what they love, and what I love

is just to lie here, listening;
swaying in the hammock
while these clouds go scudding past
and the smell of beans with garlic
wafts out through the open door.
It's the end of summer, the end, I swear,
of my last doomed love affair.
I'll spend this weekend with my friends,
these poets and kissers of my hand,
wine being poured, fog rolling in
across the dark, their voices calm.
Oh men I love, oh men I've never slept with,
calling me to eat.

Hex

I shut that black wing from my heart. That bad, bad bird. I slam the light. *Wrong love*, it flaps, *wrong love*. I slit the curtains of my eyes. If one more death makes room for one more death, I've died enough. I've died in rooms that bird screeched through, the blood-tipped feathers in my hands. The years of longing in its craw. The little claws like dangling hooks that ruined my nakedness for good. *Wrong love*, it flaps, *wrong love*. I wave my arms to make it go. As if the sky could take it back. As if my heart, that box of shadows, could be locked against itself.

1978

That winter we were so broke
we each siphoned gas from the other's car,
lived on tea and cigarettes.
You let me wear the moth-eaten mink
your last lover, the stripper, had left behind.
(Or was she a *fire-eater*, that Rose, an *exotic dancer*
heading west and sure you would follow her?
You did.) Icy mornings, I lay in bed
while you warmed both engines; the frost would melt.
The check would come in the mail any day;
you'd take me to breakfast, suddenly rich.
But while we were young and poor our breath
was visible, like steam, like smoke.
(And Rosa, your Rosa, your Rose
was the ghost in each photograph you took.
I turned from the camera, ashamed
of how my face was still unformed.)
When the snow blurred to rain you would go.
I remember the taste of gasoline
and how you wrote a few times from the road
that sullen spring, then never wrote.

Los Niños

You're not a teenage girl but you feel the heat rising off these boys. Their eyes when you enter the classroom: lowered flame; the body curves. And when you lean across a desk to whisper *good*, you smell their necks. That animal distancing itself—but not too far, still innocent. The sharp cologne they wear says *men* to you, says *almost men*. You think they have doused themselves for your sake; you straighten, swoon at their intent. At any moment they could strike the match of touch, they are that close. *Boys*, you tell yourself, *they're only boys*. And toss your head. You're thinking of wild horses, how the world will murder them.

East India Grill Villanelle

Across the table, Bridget sneaks a smile;
she's caught me staring past her at the man
who brings us curried dishes, hot and mild.

His eyes are blue, intensely blue, hot sky;
his hair, dark gold; his skin like cinnamon.
He speaks in quick-soft accents; Bridget smiles.

We've come here in our summer skirts, heels high,
to feast on fish and spices, garlic naan,
bare-legged in the night air, hot and mild.

And then to linger late by candlelight
in plain view of the waiter where he stands
and watches from the doorway, sneaks a smile.

I'd dress in cool silks if I were his wife.
We try to glimpse his hands—*no wedding band?*
The weather in his eyes is hot and mild.

He sends a dish of mango-flavored ice
with two spoons, which is sweet; I throw a glance
across the shady patio and smile.

But this can't go on forever, or all night
—or could it? Some eternal restaurant
of longing not quite sated, hot and mild.

And longing is delicious, Bridget sighs;
the waiter bows; I offer him my hand.
His eyes are Hindu blue and when he smiles
I taste the way he'd kiss me, hot and mild.

Happy Birthday, Wherever You Are

These days, if I think of you at all, to tell the truth, I don't think too hard.

Sometimes I feel ashamed I ever loved you, sometimes proud. You were too young for me, years too young, but you looked like a toppled god in bed. *Perfectly made*, I'd think; *Michelangelo's David on his side*. I'd count each rib and wait for you to wake, to stir, to live.

In the beginning, the voices were whispers I half-believed I could kiss away. Later, I wanted to press my two palms hard against your ears. As if I could shut them out. Or make you stop listening, at least.

You'd talk to that goddess over breakfast, pointing to angels in the trees. And though I'd feed you and beg you to cling fast to the known world, you would not. You shrugged on your backpack and left, one ear cocked skyward as you went.

I dreamt of you sleeping on my lawn. I took down your photographs, at last.

And then, one day, you showed up at my front door, unannounced. Said you'd walked all the way into the desert and all the way back to the city again. You looked like hell. You smelled of sweat and dust, dry wind; you stank of sun. You laughed that crazy laugh. I gave you all the cash I had.

Wherever you are now, I give you back to them, your gods. To your demons and angels and saints. To the murmur of voices inside your head. I could have held you once, I thought, and stopped you listening—for what?

Listen: I wanted to live. I wanted the wreck of your mortal beauty in my bed to keep me young. I wasn't ready for all that sky. I'm still not ready. Happy birthday. May the birds at least be kind.

Lament

First you lost the farm (some joke)
though it wasn't even yours to lose—
only your green mornings, rented,
a small house set back from a narrow road,
litters of kittens all over the porch
and your horse in the pasture, a fence.
Then you lost that handsome wreck
you'd taken in, half-rescued, rogue
who disappeared without leaving a note,
so you drowned yourself in grief for a while.
But you came back from that death, sleek
and blonde, so beautifully resurrected
that another love came along.
And then you got pregnant with twins
at forty-one, and lost both sons,
buried those two little handfuls of ash
and took up smoking again.
Now the dearest of your dogs
has lain down at your feet and won't get up—
loss upon loss upon loss
and it's the same for me, old friend.
My father, a year in the ground,
sinks every day deeper in memory,
and one doomed love just dies into the next
until every fresh beauty makes me wince.
What more can be taken? you ask
and I hear the sob catch in your throat,
the gasp of the match being struck
as you sigh, light another cigarette.
You're at your kitchen table, alone
in some northern town I've never seen;
I'm back at my mother's house in Kentucky,
out in the empty, dark garage, as far
as the telephone cord will reach.
In the distance, heat lightning, thunder—

60

an omen of summer—I listen for rain.
And I wonder how it is
we've arrived at middle age, bereft;
half of our bright lives spent
and the future a map of diminishment.
Weren't we the girls with stolen books at our hips,
our small breasts cups of milk?
Didn't we love the way we flung ourselves
blank-faced into the wind?
There's nothing to pray for anymore, you say,
as if there were miracles once,
as if there were nothing miraculous now
in the spring weather breaking, the coming storm.

The Lesser Joys

Oh, anyway, it's not the small desires that eat us up. Those little longings stirred by what—a tall man's rakish hair, the wet teeth of the bank clerk when she smiles? (Is it the heart that craves the startling brush with strangers, or the mind? A white page to lie against, blank of all history for once.) It's not the small desires that make us smaller all our lives. Illicit as they are, perhaps too seldom pounced upon. What eats us up—what leaves us bitter, bitten into, meager, mean—are the large desires still flickering when small desires have passed. The ones that haunt like childhood's trees against bare windows, bony gods. The joyless dark we fly toward, wanting what we can never have. And so I mean to make the most of what has fallen in my path. The brown-haired man, the smiling clerk, the branch I've broken from the branch. I mean you can. Give in or not. Take something like the juice of too few stars, anoint yourself.

For Mary, This Valentine's Day

There's someone else she loves
so she's gone blonde, again, and shines,
dropped thirty pounds, put down her foot,
told that tired husband (now he's sixty-six
years old—she's forty-four)
that it's too late to build the house
he said he'd build ten years ago.
There's someone else she loves
who loves her back, so there's no time
to waste unburying the past—
the teenage pregnancy that snapped her
into motherhood so young, that young
love doomed, a lover drowned, then this
old man who ran around
while she sat waiting in a trailer park.
She isn't waiting now—
she's like that girl on fire again:
the girl who was my wild big sister,
radiant and blonde, and who was lost
these many years and has returned
and paints her lips a pink I've never
seen before. I've never seen her quite
like this: a woman startled into life
at mid-life, gorgeous, lit by storms
and with that willing heart that always was
her willing heart unfurled: a banner,
that red blouse that makes it almost hurt
to look at her, to look at how
she strikes a match and tosses back
that flashy hair and rises in the smoke,
still golden, golden after all,
and nothing in this world
or any other stopping her.

Blazon

For you, I'd stick the little pins of joy in all my arms. Stitch my eyelids shut
with stars. Kiss the darkness from the dark. For you, I'd lean on wind and
let hot sky lick up my dress. My thighs a cloud through which to plunge.
My hands two prisons for your hands. For you, I'd pull the carnival of
ribbons from my heart. Commit the birdish sin of song. Float down the
river of your tongue. For you, I'd drown the wine with more wine, ruby-up
my hair. Drag strings of fish along my waist. Sigh like a heap of broken glass.
For you, I'd keep each angel in its cage of light. For you.

Hymn

He's come down for me from the trees,
come down from those gods in the branches, wind—
not a god anymore, and he breathes.

The wind rattles something below in the street,
something caught in its throat, let go of—*shhh:*
he's come down for me from the trees

and fallen beside me, lies next to me, sleeps
in the sky of his dreaming at two A.M.,
not a god anymore, and he breathes.

And I think of my father, whose death repeats
in the rattle of branches, wind's dark hymn
coming down to me from the trees.

Eternity's comfortless, some poet speaks
through the whisper of pages, *rock, hard ground,*
and no gods anymore, but he breathes

in the darkness beside me, and stirs in his dreams,
whom I've dreamed from the branches, sky, at last—
he's come down for me from the trees,
not a god anymore, and he breathes.

Provence

Brilliantly colored insects dart through the air .
. . their wings glittering in the sunlight. In
their swift, purposeful flight, they are searching
for other insects to feed on.
                                    —William A. Niering,
                                       The Life of the Marsh

He loves the smallest, least-winged things, though he might never call this love: the way he turns, barefoot, still blonde—the boy he was at pond's edge once—and calls to me, *Come look, come see.* Oh slug, oh beetle, dragonfly on which the sleek fish gorge themselves. Sunlight aswarm with what is eaten and what eats, oh hungry world. And later, in the darkness—sweet, voracious clasp and throb—we press our mouths to each small death, oh blood hum creatures that we are. I'd choose the luna moth or praying mantis, delicate and bright. He'd choose the wasp, dung beetle, ant, the most industrious and plain. If we could have another life—sucked nectar, sky-sting, kiss of muck—would we want anything so much? In sleep, he likes to touch the wing bone of my shoulder with his breath.

On Faith

How do people stay true to each other?
When I think of my parents all those years
in the unmade bed of their marriage, not ever
longing for anything else—or: no, they must
have longed; there must have been flickerings,
stray desires, nights she turned from him,
sleepless, and wept, nights he rose silently,
smoked in the dark, nights that nest of breath
and tangled limbs must have seemed
not enough. But it was. Or they just
held on. A gift, perhaps, I've tossed out,
having been always too willing to fly
to the next love, the next and the next, certain
nothing was really mine, certain nothing
would ever last. So faith hits me late, if at all;
faith that this latest love won't end, or ends
in the shapeless sleep of death. But faith is hard.
When he turns his back to me now, I think:
disappear. I think: *not what I want*. I think
of my mother lying awake in those arms
that could crush her. That could have. Did not.

How It Works

a poem is a machine made of words
—William Carlos Williams

A car is a beautiful machine. So is language. Here comes Dad. Carrying ten pounds of text and diagrams about how the engine works. I'm sixteen and this is how he thinks he's teaching me to drive. First things first. *Here's what happens when you turn the key*, he says.

Dad! The other kids are allowed to drive without understanding solenoids!

If the other kids jumped off a bridge ...? he asks. Gives me that look.

So I sit there next to him at the kitchen table, nod, *uh hum, uh hum.* Heads bowed over a book that isn't poetry—so what?

Dad's happy. Pours fresh coffee. What a girl I am. His girl.

Years later, when he's gone, I drive alone at night and listen to the engine's steady hum. The whir of pistons, cylinders; the way some spark sets off these small explosions, just like in the heart. Just like how a poem moves forward word by word by word. I think: *oh beautiful machine.* I think: *so this is how it works.*

Waking Elsewhere

I woke up dreaming my mother's garden—
fields in autumn, green turning gold,
grasses scythed down in the late, dark sun;
and here will be corn, she was saying, *tomatoes*,
flowers I never knew she loved.

I woke to a child climbing into my bed
—four-year-old girl of my sister's son—
hair like silk and the color of wheat
falling into her eyes, begging me to *get up*.

And in my mother's kitchen the strong light smelled of coffee
and autumn, in fact. In fact, my mother,
who hasn't gardened in twenty years, was taking a bath.
I heard her splashing through the walls. It was October;
the child came forward, one fresh egg cupped in her palm.

I woke up dreaming the harrowed fields,
sharp with stubble, my mother's lands.
She was already preparing for spring; she was already
stepping naked from the bath, away from grief—

a widow with work to do, weeds in the yard,
and the child calling softly to me, *come on, come on, come on.*

Late

Had I met you when I was a girl, all bony laughter and ragged sighs, I would have fallen under your shadow, knelt in the grass, been your weed, your bride. And had I met you when I was another man's wife—still young, hair full of flame—I'd have taken the spell for a sign. I'd have been jewel to your thief, little sin, and never forgiven myself for that kiss. Or had I met you in the early wind of my solitude, I might have snapped. Cracked like that naked branch I swung from all those aching, brilliant nights. Instead, you came late, you came after I'd made myself into harbor and chalice and wick. More like the ashes than any warm hearth. More like a widow than wanton, beloved. And you lifted me over the wall of the garden and carried me back to my life.

Acknowledgments

Some of these poems have appeared previously in the following publications:

Arsenic Lobster: "Grass Widow," "Hex";

Beyond Baroque: "Aubade";

The Chatahoochee Review: "Red Curtains";

The Cider Press Review: "Los Niños," "*Pour* Vivienne," "The Lesser Joys";

The Courtland Review: "Lasswade, Midlothian: Dusk";

Dogwood: "My Mother's Pillow," "Nocturne," "Ottava Rima: Lear";

Grand Passions: The Poets of Los Angeles and Beyond: "The Passionate Suitcase";

The Greensboro Review: "Waking Elsewhere";

Kalliope: "East India Grill Villanelle";

The Louisville Review: "Lament" (as "Lament for Dawn, in Spring. . .");

Natural Bridge: "Afterworld," "Après la Lune de Miel";

New Letters: "Bareback Pantoum";

Nimrod: "Provence";

Orpheus & Company: Contemporary Poets on Greek Mythology: "Hades";

Proposing on the Brooklyn Bridge: Poems about Marriage: "On Faith";

The Prose Poem: An International Journal: "Custom";

Rattle: "Blink";

Sentence: "My Mother's Birds";

Southern Poetry Review: "Dzien Dobry," "Slow Children at Play";

Water-Stone: "Forty-three Rue de Saintonge";

Quick Fiction: "Proposals."

"Last Words" borrows quotations from the poetry of Muriel Rukeyser. "Dzien Dobry" is for Sarah and Luaksz Luczaj. "The Hammock" is for Jorge Argueta and Robert Wynne. "East India Grill Villanelle" is for Bridget Kelly-Lossada. "Lament" is for Dawn Kennedy. "Waking Elsewhere" is for Victoria Paige Alberico

About the Author

Cecilia Woloch is the director of Summer Poetry in Idyllwild and a member of the MFA in Creative Writing faculty at New England College. Active in the Los Angeles literary community for more than twenty years, she has conducted poetry workshops for thousands of children, young people, and adults in venues and institutions throughout the United States and Europe, ranging from public schools and universities to prisons and hospitals. In 2003 she launched a poetry outreach program in conjunction with the Georgia Institute of Technology and Communities in Schools of Atlanta and also collaborated in the creation of International Living's first Paris Poetry Workshop. She continues to travel widely and maintains homes in both Los Angeles and Atlanta.

BOA Editions, Ltd.

AMERICAN POETS CONTINUUM SERIES

No. 1   *The Fuhrer Bunker: A Cycle of Poems in Progress*
        W. D. Snodgrass

No. 2   *She*
        M. L. Rosenthal

No. 3   *Living With Distance*
        Ralph J. Mills, Jr.

No. 4   *Not Just Any Death*
        Michael Waters

No. 5   *That Was Then: New and Selected Poems*
        Isabella Gardner

No. 6   *Things That Happen Where There Aren't Any People*
        William Stafford

No. 7   *The Bridge of Change: Poems 1974–1980*
        John Logan

No. 8   *Signatures*
        Joseph Stroud

No. 9   *People Live Here: Selected Poems 1949–1983*
        Louis Simpson

No. 10 *Yin*
        Carolyn Kizer

No. 11 *Duhamel: Ideas of Order in Little Canada*
        Bill Tremblay

No. 12 *Seeing It Was So*
        Anthony Piccione

No. 13 *Hyam Plutzik: The Collected Poems*

No. 14 *Good Woman: Poems and a Memoir 1969–1980*
        Lucille Clifton

No. 15 *Next: New Poems*
        Lucille Clifton

No. 16 *Roxa: Voices of the Culver Family*
        William B. Patrick

No. 17 *John Logan: The Collected Poems*

No. 18 *Isabella Gardner: The Collected Poems*

No. 19 *The Sunken Lightship*
        Peter Makuck

No. 20 *The City in Which I Love You*
        Li-Young Lee

No. 21 *Quilting: Poems 1987–1990*
        Lucille Clifton

No. 22 *John Logan: The Collected Fiction*

No. 23 *Shenandoah and Other Verse Plays*
        Delmore Schwartz

No. 24 *Nobody Lives on Arthur Godfrey Boulevard*
        Gerald Costanzo

No. 25 *The Book of Names: New and Selected Poems*
        Barton Sutter

No. 26 *Each in His Season*
        W. D. Snodgrass

No. 27 *Wordworks: Poems Selected and New*
        Richard Kostelanetz

No. 28 *What We Carry*
        Dorianne Laux

No. 29 *Red Suitcase*
        Naomi Shihab Nye

No. 30 *Song*
        Brigit Pegeen Kelly

No. 31 *The Fuehrer Bunker: The Complete Cycle*
        W. D. Snodgrass

No. 32 *For the Kingdom*
        Anthony Piccione

No. 33 *The Quicken Tree*
        Bill Knott

No. 34 *These Upraised Hands*
        William B. Patrick

Colophon

This edition of *Late*, Poems by Cecilia Woloch,
was set in Garamond fonts with Bernhard ModernRoman display type.
The cover was designed by Greg Boyd, Paradise, California.
The cover art, "untitled," is by Jonde Northcutt.
Manufacturing was by McNaughton & Gunn, Saline, Michigan.

The publication of this book was made possible in part by the special support of
the following individuals:

Deborah Smith-Bernstein & Martin B. Bernstein
Nancy & Alan Cameros
Ronald & Susan Dow
Dr. Henry & Beverly French
Robert & Adele Gardner
Suzanne & Gerard Gouvernet
Kip & Deb Hale
William B. Hauser
Peter & Robin Hursh
Robert & Willy Hursh
Meg Kearney
Archie & Pat Kutz
Lillian Lovelace
Donna Marbach
John & Billie Maguire
Robert & Sharon Napier
Penny & Eric Pankow
Boo Poulin
James Robie & Edith Matthai
Deborah Ronnen
Andrea & Paul Rubery
Sue Stewart
Judith Taylor
Thomas R. Ward
Pat & Michael Wilder

www.ingramcontent.com/pod-product-compliance
Lightning Source LLC
Jackson TN
JSHW080854211224
75817JS00002B/45